Wedded Bliss

The Five-Year Foundation

Jeniece Drake

Wedded Bliss: The Five Year Foundation

Copyright ©℗ 2021 Jeniece Drake| Barnett Publishing
All rights reserved.
ISBN: 978-1-7373502-7-9
ISBN-13: 9781737350279

Introduction

I've been on quite a journey in my lifetime, and the wildest parts of the ride revolve around relationships, both good and bad. I don't regret any season of my life because every experience groomed me into the woman I am today. I've become resilient, grateful, wiser, and more in tune with those around me with each encounter. Some relationships were like sandpaper; though it felt like they rubbed me the wrong way, they smoothed out my rough edges. Others entered my life like a refreshing wind and gentle rain, causing me to enter a full bloom in my spring & harvest seasons. This book is an account of how I've learned and grown from my marital encounters.

I'll be sharing insight on topics that most people tend to gloss over when preparing to spend their lives with someone. I'm taking you on a journey that'll aid you in understanding you and your spouse or soon-to-be spouse. This book is for married couples, engaged couples, and singles preparing while searching for Mrs. Right or waiting to be found by Mr. Right. Today, you're taking the first step toward laying or repairing the foundation that will uphold the legacy you and your spouse will build together.

Part One

In The Beginning

It was July of 2011; we'd just finished dinner and walked along the tree-lined path as the warm summer air kissed our faces. I'd never been so in love, never felt so complete, and never expected what was about to unfold. He turned to me with a nervous smile on his face and suggested we sail out on the lake to watch the sunset. I excitedly accepted—what better way to end a romantic day than catching the sunset on the lake. As I took in the magnificent view, I turned to ask if someone could take a picture of us. A woman immediately volunteered, and as I finished showing her how to use the camera, I turned around to him kneeling on one knee, hand in pocket. In shock and denial, I began to think maybe he's just about to tie his shoe because this is not happening right now! The ring box exited his pocket as if in slow motion. I sat frozen and in shock. He proceeded to open the box, expressed his unyielding love, and asked the question, "will you marry me?" With tears in my eyes and an enthusiastic yes, our journey to the next level began.

I immediately announced the big news, and to my surprise, I was the last to know that I would be returning from our romantic getaway with a

Wedded Bliss: The Five Year Foundation

fiancé. Everyone was ecstatic, of course, mainly because they knew my track record for turning down marriage proposals. No, he wasn't the first to ask the big question, but he was and always will be the last. Then the next big question started rolling in; when is the big day?! Being the cautious planner that I am, I chose a date two years from the time of the proposal because it would allow us ample time to pay for the wedding. My husband agreed with the logic, but I later found out he didn't want to wait that long. Without realizing that I was the one that chose the wedding date, people began to speak negatively about our relationship.

It was just the beginning, and God was already starting to show us who to shield our relationship from. This was when we would learn our first lesson as we prepared for marriage, "don't let other people into your relationship." Unfortunately, as we proudly announced our dates, people began to make negative statements that had the potential to end a marriage before it began.

"Why is he waiting two years to marry you?"

"He's not ready yet; run now."

"He just gave you that ring to make you think he's ready for commitment."

"Good job, man, get her on the hook and keep pushing the wedding out."

"Yeah, that's right, wait as long as you can and then move on."

You get the point. Do you have "friends" who would say things like this instead of praying for you or taking the time to understand the choice? If so, these are certainly not the people you'll want to confide in when you are seeking advice or in need of a good venting session. They will not offer you a Godly perspective to healing the situation. Instead, they will fan the flames and send you further into darkness. What people failed to understand was that I was the one that decided to wait two years. Therefore, their comments were incorrect. Unfortunately, constantly hearing those words took its toll on both of us. We began to think that our decision, while best for us, was incorrect. About three months after the engagement, my then fiancé asked to move the wedding up to July 2012 instead of 2013. A strong desire to shut the naysayers up led me to agree without fully thinking through the consequence of the decision. My leisurely prep time turned into a mad dash to the altar as I picked up extra hours at work, worked to maintain my 4.0 GPA in school, and spent days running back and forth between Brooklyn and Long Island. Can you say exhausted?!

I enjoyed the look on people's faces when I revealed that I was the one that set the original date, and my fiancé had now moved up the wedding because he didn't feel the need to wait. Moreover, I did not enjoy the fast-paced preparations and the extra workload to pay off the wedding. Thankfully, I wasn't alone; I had some close friends and family that helped pick up the slack where needed. So, what was the real problem? In the haste to plan my perfect day, we were neglecting our planning for the perfect marriage! We were two imperfect people about to journey into the unknown, with no clue as to how we would spiritually become one.

Yeah, we read all the books and the bible references, combed through Song of Solomon, but come on, you know as well as I know that reading and application are not the same things. With about four to five months left before we headed to the altar, we had no time to spare to start counseling. Some of you may be groaning and swearing at this stage, but statistics show that couples that go through marriage counseling are more likely to stay married than those that do not. Why? They are better equipped to deal with the rocky road ahead. They learn how to fix what's broken as opposed to throwing it in the trash!

Let's discuss some things that may come up during counseling that you may not consider during the hype of wedding planning.

What does marriage mean to you?

Each of you needs to sit down with paper and a pen to write your definition of what it means to commit. Think about all of the people you met throughout your life. Out of all the people you could have chosen to spend your life with, what made you choose him/her? Ponder on what attracted you to each other, what unique qualities does your husband or future husband possess that screamed: "that's the one." What about him or her makes you believe that they possess what it takes to help shape you into the person you desire to be? Then talk to each other about what you have written.

Not only will you be getting a head start on your vows, but you'll also learn something new about him or her and their vision of the commitment you two are about two make to one another. If you're already married and going through a rough patch, this will help bring back the memory of why you are together in the first place, bringing you one step closer to reconciliation.

Marriage is more than the wedding day and more important than the size of the ring he bought. When one of you makes a huge mistake, which both of you will, it'll be too easy to take that ring off and throw it across the room. That rock on your finger won't be there to give you the support you need to get through tough times. It won't keep you from hurting one another. That ring does one thing: lets the world know that you are off-limits and nothing more. You'll need to know that you and your spouse can choose to love each other even when you don't feel like it. Your commitment and investment in your marriage need to be more than material to ensure survival.

How will you join your finances together?

Have you two discussed and agreed to complete financial disclosure and discussed your pre-marital debt? Talk about arrangements that will be made when it comes to bank accounts? These are just a few issues that should be discussed before the wedding to ensure everyone is on the same page. You'll also want to sit down and talk about your and your spouse's expectations regarding how you'll pay off debt incurred before marriage. Speaking from my experience, my husband and I found it easier to add our debt to our monthly budget and just pay it all off together. He didn't file for my student loans, and I didn't charge anything on his credit cards, but

Wedded Bliss: The Five Year Foundation

we are in this together, and it seemed fitting that we worked as a team to get out of debt.

Many couples choose the 50/50 approach, tallying up the monthly bills to split the cost down the middle. This works well for roommates, but you two are to become one. That's 100% of the husband and 100% of the wife; there is no separation! For those of you saying, "I want my money to do what I want without big brother watching," there is a solution for you without going against the spiritual order of things. Start a joint bank account in which both of your checks will be directly deposited each pay period. Use this account for all household bills, groceries, medical bills, and any other household necessity. Based on your budget, place the agreed-upon amount into your savings accounts and place the agreed-upon amounts in your individual accounts, something like an allowance for each of you that you'll add to each pay period. This will ensure that all bills are paid in a timely fashion, and when you two are spending on lunch or gifts for one another, neither of you will cut into the bill money. You will also still be able to surprise your spouse with gifts from time to time or on special occasions.

You'll also want to talk about things like:

- o Using a financial planner
- o Saving for retirement
- o Whether you will have a two-income household
- o Will your children be attending public or private school?
- o College tuition for your children
- o Tax preparation
- o How you plan on resolving issues that arise concerning finances.

This is a subject that often throws newlyweds off, and it will benefit you both to take some time to sit down and talk about the best way to handle this. The two of you know and understand your aspirations better than anyone, so as you read this, I pray that the Holy Spirit reveals the best course of action for God's plan concerning your union. May His providing hand be over your finances, may you be blessed with more than enough, an overflow that will benefit the nations and draw others to the grace, glory, and perfection that is the Godly union of His children.

What are your love languages?

Alright, you might have just turned your head sideways, asking yourself, "what the heck is a love language." There are five love languages:

Words of Affirmation – A person that falls into this category is more likely to feel loved when he or she is given voluntary compliments. Just hearing the words "I love you" are enough to make his or her day. While loving words will send this person over the moon, negative comments are brutally painful and will not be easily forgotten.

Quality Time – This person desires one's undivided attention to feel loved. To appease someone that speaks this love language, there can be no distraction when communicating with them. That means T.V. off and phones down; your spouse should be your only focus at the time. Rescheduling dates and interrupting when you should be listening will leave your spouse heartbroken if this is their love language.

Wedded Bliss: The Five Year Foundation

Receiving Gifts – Please know that this does not mean that you can simply buy your spouse a gift, and they'll just walk away feeling loved. For someone with this love language, the gift giver must put a great deal of thought, love, and effort into the gift. In doing so, the receiver of the gift will feel loved and cared for. They will feel as though they are genuinely appreciated and valued. For someone with this love language, be sure not to miss special dates like birthdays and anniversaries, and don't forsake the value of taking the time to show their value to you daily.

Acts of Service – Are there chores that need to be done around the house? If this is your spouse's love language, then cleaning the dishes without having to be asked will be like screaming "I love you" from a mountain top for all the world to hear. So that nagging spouse that says, why can't you just help me around the house is saying, "why don't you love me?"

Physical Touch – Nope, this doesn't mean you'll be in the bedroom all day, but hey, that could be fun too. This language is about types of touches that convey positive messages, such as a pat on the back, hugs, holding hands, etc. This person would find physical abuse and neglect unforgivable.

It is crucial to understand how to communicate love to your spouse and how your spouse may be attempting to express their love for you. Early in our relationship, my husband would buy things to make me happy; though I appreciated the gesture, it just wasn't conveying the message he hoped it would. He was trying to show me that he loved me, but I remained unfulfilled. It was a frustrating time for both of us. He began to feel unappreciated, and I felt unloved, and this could have been avoided if we understood each other's love language. Once he understood that quality time was the way to my heart, things began to go smoother in that area of our relationship.

Now, one's definition of quality time may differ from person to person, but as mentioned above, it will always include shutting everything else down and giving your spouse your undivided attention. In my case, quality time involved a time for the two of us to talk about our day, share things that God has revealed to us or promises that had come to fruition, praying together, Bible study, and even listening to a sermon and discussing our revelations after. It took time to strengthen our relationship with God together; that really made the most significant impact on our relationship. Husbands, without submission to God, your wife will find it near impossible to submit or trust you. It's not enough to quote the scripture to your wife and expect her to bow down and lead her astray from God's path for your family. God will not allow your kingdom woman to follow you if you are not following His instructions. Wives, your husbands are not perfect, and imperfection is not a reason to assume the head of household. If you see him struggling in his duties, this is your chance to pray and ask God how you can help him; never forget that you are his helpmeet!

As our pastor once said, "the husband is the thermostat, and the wife is the thermometer." As head of the household, the husband will set the spiritual temperature for the family, and the behaviors or actions of one's wife will show the temperature. In other words, if your household is not in order and running cold in the spirit, it's time to check in with The Father, man of God. When things are running smoothly in the household, everyone's needs are being met, and everyone's spiritual life is on track; the heat and passion you get from your woman of God will let you know you're headed in the right direction. There will be ups and downs in every marriage, your ability to stand together, love one another, and cover each other in prayer during the storm will determine just how far you'll make it together.

Take this time to declare even now: "My marriage is not a phase. It's not a pit stop. Our love is forever. It's forged in the very image of The King of Kings. We will stand on His foundation, fight for one another, be a refuge to each other, prosper together, and cherish one another in Jesus mighty name. Amen!"

What are your personality types?

Is either of you an introvert or extravert, sensing or intuitive, more prone to thinking or feeling, more likely to judge or perceive? While I won't go into too much detail here, there are 16 personality types, and understanding your spouse's will pave the way for greater communication and overall positive interactions with one another. Just think about it; you wouldn't plan a huge birthday bash for an introverted spouse. He or she would most likely enjoy an intimate gathering of close family and friends or a relaxing spa day topped off with a romantic dinner for two. Understanding each other's personalities allows you a more intimate connection with your spouse, affording you a deeper, more meaningful relationship over the years. The better you know each other, you'll find it difficult for people to come between the two of you.

Wedded Bliss: The Five Year Foundation

You two may have particular quirks that others find unacceptable in a relationship. Still, because you know each other more intimately, these peculiarities may be endearing to you or something you can handle because you understand why they exist. The only being that understands your spouse better than you is God, and if that's not true, then you two have some serious connecting to do. Now is the time to groom yourselves for the next level. The level of understanding it took to be a boyfriend or girlfriend will not suffice once you step into the roles of husband and wife. That takes a fresh anointing, self-awareness, the armor of God, and a level of endurance that you've never experienced before. No worries, let's warm up those cold feet; God is ready, willing, and able to provide the tools necessary to bring greatness into and from your union. Don't forget that your marriage is a ministry. When you two are joined together as one there will be major opposition, but the things you accomplish together will bring Glory to God and set others free into the Kingdom.

I'm getting excited for you guys. There is something in you that the world needs. God has chosen you to come together for a purpose that will further his Kingdom. Perhaps you will be the vessels that will raise up the next great man or woman of God, the next president, the next leader that will take Mankind to new heights. Maybe you're going to be a beacon of hope to other struggling couples. No matter the plan, rejoice and have good faith. You're on your way to greatness, and you're going to look good together getting there!

Have you two discussed your life goals?

Wedded Bliss: The Five Year Foundation

Before my husband and I got married, I expressed to him my desire to leave behind a legacy, launch my own business, and find a way to give back to the community. This meant that I needed a husband who would be comfortable with having a wife working often, would be willing to handle bills when or if my businesses had a slow month, and that understood that my legacy would be OUR legacy. He expressed great excitement about these things, but it's one thing to talk about it and another to experience it. Though I felt as if I'd done an excellent job explaining what hardships may arise from my desire to be a business owner, I neglected to see that he was caught up in the hype of what life would be like once I achieved success.

Lavish spending became an issue as he equated new contracts with more money in the house. We even came to a point where he became lax in his duties as a husband because he felt I should be able to handle everything in the household. While this angered me greatly and caused a significant amount of strife between us, I had to take a step back and try to understand why he was behaving this way when he told me that he would back all my goals.

It turns out I didn't do a well enough job explaining the ins and outs of how a business is run or how long the money would have to be cycled back into the business before I could pull down a salary for myself. You see, when you two take the time to sit and talk about these things, really take the time to sit down and help each other understand what going for and reaching these goals means for each individual. Don't just highlight all the good things and gloss over the things that could go wrong. Share the fears that come with it, the potential failures and hardships that will arise, talk about these things with the same level of depth that you would speak about the high points of attaining the goal. This is your chance to prepare each other mentally and spiritually for the road that lays ahead.

What are your mutual expectations?

This is something that tends to trip couples up early on within marriage. Neither of you is a mind reader. Therefore, you can't assume that your spouse knows what you expect unless you clearly articulate it. Now is the time to sit with your partner and talk about your expectations regarding emotional support during times of sickness, loss, good times, and bad times. Come up with your plan on whether you'll be spontaneous about spending time together or planning times to catch up and have fun. This may not sound like something a passionate couple would have to talk about but trust me, it is. Our lives can get hectic, and we can get caught up with deadlines at work, children, and the list goes on. Since you will be living together, it is easy to mistake being in the same household as spending time with one another; for clarity, it is NOT.

I'll use myself as an example; I once told a co-worker that I was excited to leave for the day because it was date night. We'd only been married for a month, so it was unheard of for a newlywed to have a scheduled date night. She immediately told me that's not a good sign. I didn't feel the need to explain myself to her, but I will share it with you all. After our wedding, I was still a full-time student and in senior year. As a full-time employee, student, full-time wife, and part-time entrepreneur, it was vital that I didn't allow my busy schedule to keep me from my husband. What outsiders viewed as a marriage destined for failure was a marriage destined to bloom. My husband was understanding of my busy schedule, but he was in awe of the fact that I never let my schedule keep me from making sure dinner was ready when he got home and spending quality time with him. To this day, he finds it remarkable, and it brings us closer each day.

Another good topic of discussion is whether you two will have a two-income household and whether one of you will stay home once kids enter the picture. Initially, I couldn't see myself as a stay-at-home mom. I thought that I would go insane trying to find things to do. Well, one child later and I tip my hat to stay at home mothers, you all rock! So, my husband and I discussed that we would be a two-income household; however, my income would not always come from salaried employment. We also agreed that by the time we had our first child, I would already be working from home, which would cut down on childcare. This plan was not without its challenges, but we managed. Had we not talked about these things, my husband would have been blindsided, which would have been a disaster.

Some of you may be in a predicament where one may make more money than the other. You two will want to sit down discuss how you both feel about the situation. Does one feel inferior to the other, does he/she feel insecure, or will there be an expectation of the spouse that makes less to find a position that pays more money. Whatever the case may be, do not enter your marriage without a clear understanding of each other's expectations. If you're already married, fret not; you can still sit down and have this discussion, devise a plan of action, and move forward. You only have forever together; you'll get it down.

Will you have children? If so, how many?

One of the worst things you want to do is get married with a dream of hearing the pitter-patter of little feet, only to realize that your spouse never wanted kids. This is a must-have conversation! You're pledging to live your lives together; you don't want to force the man or woman you love into an undesired position. In some cases, after marriage, one spouse may convince the other that children will be a great idea; however, this will depend heavily on why they do not desire children. Are the two of you on the same page about starting a family with one another? Awesome! You two need to talk about how many children you will have. This can be a touchy subject in some cases.

My husband and I agreed that we wanted two children, and we were content with that. I began to have second thoughts about limiting the number of children because I wasn't sure how I felt about birth control as a kingdom woman. This can be a difficult decision for many couples. The Lord commissioned us to be fruitful and multiply, so the question arises: am I limiting God when placing a number on the number of children we will have. Yet still, we have a duty not to live beyond our means as well; we would be putting too much of a burden on ourselves financially, mentally, physically, and spiritually if we had more children than we could handle. Moments like these are why we put everything out on the table, put it before God, and pray earnestly for guidance.

We may not have all the answers when we have these talks, but it gets you thinking. It brings the two of you before God together, strengthening your spiritual and physical relationship. Trust God that just as He brought you both together, He will get you through it together as well.

Parents & In-laws:

It's easy to get caught up in the excitement that you found the love of your life, your best friend, and now you're going to spend the rest of your life together. Well, don't forget that your beautiful union will also bring you a new set of parents. Things to consider when talking about your in-laws are:

- The amount of time you'll each spend with your parents and the amount of time you'd like your spouse to be part of that
- Holiday arrangements
- Parental expectations during the holiday and how they'll be handled
- Whether you two are comfortable with sharing marital issues with parents
- The relationship your kids will have with their grandparents
- Should your or your spouse's parents fall into financial hardship, will it be ok to help them out

- Are you comfortable with a parent moving in with you when they grow old?

Relationships with one's in-laws can be hit or miss. Some may luck out, and everyone loves each other. Some will have to wait for their in-laws to warm up to them, and others will be in for a whacky ride, to say the least, but if you talk about it now, the ride won't be as bumpy. This is also a great time to learn more about your in-laws in hopes of connecting with them better. Who knows how to woo them better than their child? My parents adored my husband from the beginning. My in-laws had to warm up to me; he's the baby of the family, so they were very protective. I'm delighted to say we all get along better now that they've gotten the chance to learn who I am, and I was given the golden opportunity to learn more about them and how to communicate with them effectively as well. God is good all the time!

Gender role expectations:

Gone are the days of traditional gender roles. Some men have grown up only seeing their mothers as the head of household, and some women grew up with dads that cooked, cleaned, and raised them. It's NOT safe to assume that your spouse will just fall into a particular role simply because he was born a man or she was born a woman. Currently, household chores are often shared, but if this is not familiar to you due to how you were raised, you should make that known. I once had someone's wife tell me that she doesn't clean the bathroom because she was taught that it's a man's job. So, if someone is slacking on a household chore, you may want to ask why before flying off the handle. Discuss how you two would like to split the household responsibilities. It's your household, so you can do what works best for you two.

You'll also want to consider the following:

- Who will be expected to stay home when the children are sick?
- Do you both plan to work when you have children
- Do you have a preference on what you'd rather do to contribute to the household?

There are also spiritual gender roles that must be considered and, in some cases, taught, which is why I recommend marriage counseling. We all know that the man is head and the woman is to follow, but this does not mean that the husband can walk all over his wife and do whatever he wants. As a husband, you must be so in tune with God that every decision you make follows the will of God. If you're paying attention, I just taught you how to keep your wife from knit-picking every decision you make. Let me repeat it when you come to a fork in the road, and you're trying to decide whether to go left or right, and you go right, it better be because you heard the voice of God give the direction. She can fight with you all day but rest assured she can't fight with God. What does this mean for a wife? When you submit to your husband, you are submitting to God. When your husband brings you a plan, you will be who he needs to help him build it. You will build and nurture the children, your legacy, and your future. You will be the one that picks up the pieces and reflects his true strength when the world tears him down, you woman of God, are his earthly strength and the glue that will hold him together. He is incomplete until God releases you to him, so it is in his best interest to cater to you, ensure your happiness and spiritual well-being. Without you, he will not be able to please God or fulfill his destiny. Though you two have entirely different roles, what you both bring to the table is equally important. One is not and cannot be less than the other because you are one flesh. **To claim superiority over your spouse is to claim inferiority in oneself.**

How will you resolve heated conflicts?

Every healthy relationship has its heated moments, tempers flare, things get said, and you two take time out from one another to cool off before making up. Getting married means living together and spending a day or two apart because you're mad can do more damage than good. This is not to say that you're not entitled to time to yourself, you certainly are, but there is a reason why the Bible instructs us not to allow the sun to set on our anger. Doing so allows the enemy to plant thoughts in your mind that was never there. Imagine this; you're unpacking the bags after returning from the market together. You remember telling your spouse to pick up the milk, a household staple; your spouse promises that they got everything you asked for. When you're done, you realize there's no milk; you proceed to scold your spouse for it. By the end of your tirade, you're both extremely upset and storm off to different parts of the house. Neither of you is about to apologize, and so you begin to play the whole thing over in your mind repeatedly. Now you're thinking of snappy comebacks you should have said. Each time you calm down, you relive it again, the anger welling up inside you, burning hotter and hotter. Now you can't even stand the sight of each other, so you decide to sleep in separate rooms. If left unchecked, something as simple as forgetting milk turns into you never listen to me, this is why..., and all of a sudden, you're bringing up stuff from 10 years ago, or you start bringing up things that had nothing to do with the initial argument. You may laugh, but it happens.

If one of you had the humility to give it over to God, come to each other to acknowledge where you both went wrong, listened to each other's ideas about how to keep this from happening again, and prayed together, you would be able to avoid a huge blow out over "spilled milk." My husband and I have a rule that we have to come to an agreement concerning how a matter will be handled. We understand that we know we'll have to talk about what issues came up between us at some point in the day. Some sort of compromise that allows us to close the day together must be met. The subject may remain open while we figure out how to work it out, but the anger behind it must be released, and our love must shine through above it. We also agree not to throw past situations in each other's faces. Once an issue is closed or resolved, that's the end of it. If we discuss past issues, it's as a remembrance so we can see how far we've come since then and celebrate the strength forged from it.

Conflicts are not an easy thing to handle within a marriage, but you and your spouse, with the guidance of God and other kingdom-minded married couples, will make it through stronger than the day you stood before each other and said, "I do."

What are your thoughts concerning the sexual relationship of your marriage?

Sex in marriage is often glossed over in the church and not particularly thought of outside of the church either. People simply regard it as "legal sex." Once married, no one can judge you for what you do in your bedroom or the children resulting from those intimate moments. In your mind, you two may be thinking, ok, how difficult is this? We're official; we just jump in bed and do what we do. Well, as with all other intricate parts of a marriage, there is more my friend.

You two may want to discuss how often you each expect to have intimate nights or days together. When concerns do arise about a spouse's sex drive, how will you two approach it? Depending on the situation, this can be a sensitive subject, so you'll want to be gentle and choose your words wisely during these discussions. This would also be an excellent time to discuss when what sexual activities are off-limits or fantasies you may have.

Here's something else you most likely didn't consider, what happens to the sex drive during pregnancy, and what could happen after the baby arrives. In the beginning, all was well, and neither of us had complaints about our intimacy levels. Once we started our family, that is when the struggle arose, and let me tell you, it can just sneak up on you! At first, you don't think anything of it because you two are walking zombies. New baby equals no sleep AT ALL. I've concluded that babies are so darn cute because God wants to distract us from how hard it is to raise them. For months, my husband and I were at odds with each other, and it had a lot to do with the fact that we were so focused on our daughter and everything else going on around us, we'd forgotten about our intimate time. For a married couple, sexual relations are times to bond on another level. We are joined both physically and spiritually during this time, providing a mutual pleasure only shared between husband and wife. In some moments resulting in the creation of a new life, it's a fragile and sacred moment and something that God takes pride & pleasure in as we engage in the fruits of our union.

Before you move on to the next chapter, take some time to reflect on the things you've learned not just from your reading but from and about each other. Talk to each other about the new revelations that have been revealed to you. Share your plans with one another and begin to build a genuine excitement and the start of your plan for your journey together.

Part Two

The Foundation

There is beauty and purpose in a God-designed marriage, but it takes patience, endurance, and focus to see it clearly. Each spouse is unique and brings something different to the table; each should be giving 100% of themselves to achieve their God-ordained purpose. Both need to be firmly rooted in the foundation of God while being watered and nurtured in a continuous flow of the Holy Spirit.

I want you to sit in a quiet place and imagine you're sitting in a classroom. Your vision clouded as you attempt to understand the focus of the lesson;

you're unprepared, unfocused, and can't understand what the teacher is writing on the board. You realize that everyone around you seems to understand what's going on. They're nodding their heads, taking notes, and absorbing all the information given. You, on the other hand, are dazed and confused. You'll look up toward the front of the room as a student digging through his bag catches your attention. He pulls out a pencil, hands it to a student behind him, and they continue to pass on the pencil until it reaches you. Just as you're attempting to take notes, you realize you have no book; at that moment, a young lady sitting next to you places a book on your desk. You're all set, but you still lack clear sight; everything on the board looks fuzzy. You then turn to look out the window attempting to focus your vision. As you work to focus on the images outside, you begin to see past the fog, through the mess of the world, and behold the beauty of the gardens and trees that line the school's campus. With a renewed sight, you prepare yourself for the lesson of the day, excited and eager to gain new knowledge.

This, ladies and gentlemen, is what marriage looks and feels like as your eyes begin to adjust after the blinders come off. There's no longer a way to hide your flaws, and you're both about to learn what it really means to love each other for better or worse. Though you've taken the time to learn as much as you could about each other before the ceremony, as much as you could about marriage, there's always going to be something new that comes up. Learning how to do something from a textbook is one thing, but it's a whole other ballgame to apply those lessons. In a class and in a book, we learn in a controlled setting that's free of unbridled emotions and eager-like minds soaking up information. In theory, everything you take in will work if I just do it like they say in the book. If I just follow the teacher's rules, everything will work out, and you begin to settle into this false sense of security. However, once you've graduated and been deemed knowledgeable to now apply your education in life ahead, you find that the world you've been launched into is messy, it's a cruel teacher, and many times you'll have to think on your feet and alter or tailor those lessons you learned to successfully navigate through life.

Remember those two students that gave you the pencil and the book so you'd have the necessary tools to make your time in class more effective? God will send people to help equip you with the tools you need to make your time together more effective, but if you don't take the time to adjust your focus properly, you will miss the blessing and become stuck in a rut because you missed the opportunity to receive and write down the lesson that God was teaching for the day. When we focus on the things we don't like about our spouse, we miss the lesson on how to love unconditionally. If your focus is on all the things that your spouse doesn't do, then you miss the lesson on how to help build your spouse by teaching them a few tricks for time management. We can't focus on all the mess that our human flesh brings into the household. We must adjust our vision and remain focused on why God brought us together, note each other's weaknesses and then step up to utilize our strengths to pick up where our spouses may drop the ball. Be gentle with one another, understanding, and supportive when one faces any type of failure. How you respond will set the atmosphere for healing and respect or dread and contempt. When faced with a dilemma that will require a soft tongue while the heat of anger tries to burn its way out, pull out a scripture that reminds you of your God nature.

Take a deep breath, release, and say…

"Put on then, as God's chosen ones, holy and beloved, compassionate hearts, kindness, humility, meekness, and patience. – Colossians 3:12 ESV

It's ok to remind yourself who you are, whose you are, and why you've been chosen for this journey. In fact, doing so will keep you focused on the goal God has placed before you. Press toward the mark family; you're going to make it in Jesus name!

Balance and Order

Let all things be done decently and in order.
1 Corinthians 14:40

It is vital to strive daily to attain and maintain balance in your household. It may seem difficult and, in some cases, impossible, but it will take a team effort, and you'll have to do it even on days that you don't like each other very much. Trust me, those of you who believe that will never happen, humanity always trips us up, and becoming husband and wife does not transform us into super-humans. You're about to find out which part of your spouse was the act to win your heart and which parts were the real deal. Despite what troubles may come, your decision to love one another and hold your vows will be critical to your success.

Your marriage is more than just your love and respect for each other; it's a ministry. A kingdom marriage is like a beacon of hope to those that have been broken, seeking relationships out of order. You are the example of what it looks like when love has been awakened in a timely matter. Many have been broken by their illegal entry into the sacred realm of marriage. Remember it is what God puts together that no man can break apart; therefore, if you awaken the dimension of love in your life before God has released you, there will be a war in the spirit that you are not equipped or mature enough to handle.

Premature Love ~vs.~ Mature Love

I charge you, O daughters of Jerusalem, that ye stir not up,
nor awake my love until he pleases.
Song of Solomon 8:4

When I first heard this scripture, I understood it to mean that you shouldn't be in an intimate relationship before you're ready, but after marriage, I truly understand the meaning of this warning. When I was young and foolish, I knew it all, or so I thought. Desperate to get out of my parents' house, I made the rashest decision I've ever made in my life. After years of telling men who wanted to marry me that they were crazy and I didn't want a husband, I used one of these men to get an apartment.

At the time, I was serving as a minister in church, and shacking up wasn't appealing to me as I desperately wanted to please God. However, blinded by my desire to be the queen of my household, I accepted the marriage proposal of a man I knew in my heart was not meant for me. Heck, my head and heart were on the same page, but I saw my way out of what I viewed as parental jail, so I took my chances. Of course, my mother disapproved of this union, my father told him that he didn't think he was ready to handle his daughter, and we were met with opposition from all angles, but I just kept telling myself, if I'm married to the man I'm living with no one could judge me. This is a prime example of what man put together as opposed to what God joins together.

What I failed to realize was that I was illegally entering a realm of ministry that I wasn't ready for, and I was ultimately allowing my desire to break free from parental control to blind me from what God really wanted me to do. People, I don't care what you tell yourself, know this, trying to apply biblical principles to your life in a way that benefits you yet takes you further from fulfilling your life's purpose is always going to end in heartache. In this scenario, I had become Jonah, and the man I had agreed to marry was my whale. The word of God is not ours to twist and mold to fit our wants or desires but rather a guide that helps us navigate life as we submit to the will of the Father. It isn't easy, but it's a necessity.

From day one, that union was doomed, and there was nothing I could do about it. I traded a loving, supportive home, with rules I thought were unfair, for a lying, sneaky, underhanded mate that made my life a living hell. But God still saw fit to give me hope. Though I now would have to reap what I had sown, I was still granted grace and mercy. This time in my life should have ended in either my death or life incarceration, but God stepped in and covered me despite going against His will. What the enemy means for evil, God will always turn around for our Good. God turned the tables and used me in such a mighty way that it blew me away when I'd realized what he'd done.

This man that I committed myself to was a wolf in sheep's clothing. Though he served as a pastor in the church, he stole money from our household, drank like a lush, smoked weed, and God only knows what else as he would often go missing for hours without a word from him. I'd gotten myself into quite the pickle. After 2 to 3 months, I realized that I married a man that would pray on women in the church, drive them insane, leave them with nothing, and mentally broken, acting as if he were the victim in the relationship. All glory be to God; when he met me, he met his match!

So many women in the church hated me during this time but little did they know that me taking this position had literally saved them from being torn apart! This was one of the most trying times of my spiritual walk. It took daily prayer for release and repentance to maintain my sanity. I just had to believe that God wouldn't punish me forever for this bonehead move. At one point, it got so bad that I began to fear for my life, so I slept with the bedroom door locked with a kitchen knife to defend myself if the need arose. Afraid that if he were to attack me and I used a weapon, I would more than likely end up the one in jail under such a corrupt system, I moved my family pit bull into the house as extra protection because I knew he would protect me at all cost!

Around this time, I decided that I would no longer live in fear but devote every waking moment to God, school, and work. This decision saved my life, and I began to finally move forward again, I gained the ear of church leadership, and the tables had finally begun to turn back in my favor. The

Wedded Bliss: The Five Year Foundation

Holy Spirit would always keep me one step ahead of him. His tricks no longer irritated or affected me. It was blowing his mind that he couldn't break me as he had so many women before me. His misdeeds had been revealed as God allowed me a platform to shed light on what he was really doing to me and what he had been doing to other women in the church.

Let me tell you, God may cover sin for a season as He gives you a chance to get it together, but if you continue down the wrong path, He'll eventually expose you for who you are. At some point, you will have to answer for what you've done to His children, and when the time comes to pay up, you better believe it's going to be painful, and that fall is going to hurt something fierce. The people that man turned against me eventually had to come back to me and ask forgiveness. Nobody but the Lord can make that happen.

I'll never forget the day that God rewarded me for my faithfulness and broke me free of the hell my decision had brought me. It was summer, school had just let out, and my mother wanted to take my brother on vacation to Disney as a graduation present. I didn't have the cash, but my mother paid my way because she believed I needed a break from the mess. It was nice to get away, and I had a blast for the week that we were away but little did I know God was moving me out of the way and working in my favor at home.

Drum roll, please....

When I got back from Florida, I arrived home to find it completely cleared, and he was nowhere in sight. I called him to find out what was going on, and he told me that he's moved out and he was leaving me. Cue the praise break!!! I immediately had him stop by to sign over his rights to the apartment and had the landlord draw up a new lease. I know what some of you may be thinking. How could you be happy after he took everything from the house? Here's my perspective, I can replace things, but I can't get back lost time, my life, or my sanity should I have been stuck with such a man for the rest of my natural life. To top it off, God blessed me so that I would be able to keep my apartment. Yes, that's right. I went about it the wrong way, I paid a hefty price for it, but God still gave me my apartment!

So, what does this have to do with not awakening love until it so desires? My illegal entry into the realm of marriage took me into a level of warfare that I wasn't ready for. Mentally, physically, and spiritually I was not mature enough to take on the role of a wife, just as he wasn't prepared to take on the role of a husband. Though divorce is frowned upon in the church, God persuading him to leave me opened the door for me to continue my spiritual journey and grow into the woman of virtue that would someday be the helpmeet to His kingdom man of choice. Even though I walked through that door to move forward in my journey with God, I was not left unscathed by the ordeal. The damage suffered robbed me of the desire to share my life with another. At this point in my life, all I wanted was God and me, and I considered adopting a child later in life. Stepping into a relationship as sanctified and holy as marriage before your ordained time will hurt your chances at embracing and submitting to a God-filled union.

Past relationships leave us with baggage consisting of insecurities that are not the fault of our present companion. Many times, it's these insecurities that rear their ugly heads during our marriages, and we find ourselves fighting with our spouses about things that honestly have nothing to do with them. If we can't be naked before our spouse, then we have not fully committed to the relationship. I don't mean nude in the physical sense, but utterly transparent with nothing hidden from our spouse. We should walk in our marriages completely naked and unashamed. Previous relationships are equivalent to the fruit given to Adam & Eve in the garden. As we continued to eat the fruits of the wrong companionships, our eyes were opened to shame, and we began to hide ourselves. In comes the proverbial brick wall that must be broken down before marriage. Now, like Mankind's first husband and wife, you must work hard and toil in pain to yield good fruits in your marriage.

God clearly told me that my husband was under construction and that he was someone that I went to high school with. Even with that information, I did my best to block it out of my mind and keep living my life with only God as my head. I must admit that though I had some trying moments, this was an easier time. Only being responsible for myself makes decision-making easier, but having that time alone also helped me understand myself more, which, oddly, put me in the prime position to learn how to be a kingdom woman and wife. Isn't God funny?!

A Husband Finds His Wife

*He who finds a wife finds a good thing
and obtains favor from the Lord*

Wedded Bliss: The Five Year Foundation

Proverbs 18:22

Every man is born with a purpose, and for every man, there is a woman equipped to meet their needs. Women are the pillars that hold the covering, the husband, which is why a man finds a good thing and why we shouldn't step into that role before our God-appointed time. The Bible also says that husbands receive the favor of the Lord, meaning he approves and supports the union. In Genesis 2:18-25, the reason God designed marriage is revealed.

Adam was given dominion over the earth was told to name every creature therein. Each creature was paraded before Adam during the naming process, and as commissioned, he named them. They were presented to him one male and one female, every creation with a mate, but there stood Adam, the most loved of all created, yet he stood alone. Nowhere on the earth was there a companion for God's beloved, and so He created woman from Adam's rib, thus the reason we are considered one flesh after marriage. At this point, the perfect man became but a fraction of himself as some qualities were removed and bestowed upon the new creation, his companion, Eve.

There were times that I would look at my husband baffled as to why he couldn't do certain things until one day I realized that my areas of weakness are his strengths and vice versa. When God made two beings from the same flesh, our skill sets were divided as well. This forces us to acknowledge that we need one another to be complete. Since we were made in the image of God, it's only right that our union would mirror the creator. The Holy Trinity and the trinity of marriage mirror each other.

Wedded Bliss: The Five Year Foundation

The three of us are one! To disrespect your spouse is not only to disrespect yourself, but ultimately, you'll be dishonoring God in the process.

Reflection of The Holy Trinity

The Father	God
The Son	The Husband
The Holy Spirit	The Wife

Husbands love your wives

Husbands, love your wives, even as Christ also loved the church, and gave himself for it
Ephesians 5:25 KJV

For God so loved the world that he gave His only begotten son so that the world through him may be saved (John 3:16). Husbands, what are you willing to sacrifice to protect your wife? We believe that God and the Son are one; therefore, God laid down His life for His beloved creation. The husband is God's earthly covering for the woman he's been given charge over. This does not mean that he's in control of his wife, but by right, he is the ordained head of the household. The man that loves his wife as Christ loves the church values her more than his own life. He understands that without this woman by his side, failure is inevitable. She's the most valuable treasure of all he possesses. She's irreplaceable; her light brightens his day, her breath is his breath, her pain is his pain, her sorrow is his sorrow, and her joys his joy. When a man's wife is provided for, secure, happy, and at peace, the same is true for the husband.

Imagine you've just had the most challenging day at work. Everything that could go wrong did. It's as if the bottom fell out, and you hit a downward spiral that seems to have no end. You come home, and your wife greets you with a warm smile; the house is clean, dinner is ready, and suddenly a sense of peace falls over you. When your wife is secure, knowing she can trust you to lead, that frees her to move in her role effortlessly to be everything you need to renew your spirit after a day of working to provide. When her needs are met, she can meet your need with no problem because she isn't scrambling to find what she needs to make the day run smoothly.

Meeting these needs as God met the need of the church means be her provider. Yes, you may be a two-income household, and there's nothing wrong with that, but I'm sure your wife has emotional needs that must be met daily that offer her the security she needs to be your helpmeet at all times. An emotionally drained woman running off fumes will be of no use to you on your journey. When your car starts sputtering, you know it's time to gas it up. Well, when your wife's tank is on "E," it's time to step up and refuel her, or you're both going to be stranded. There's nothing worse than feeling stuck because your spouse neglected their duties.

The Proverbs 31 Woman

Who can find the virtuous woman?
For her price is far above rubies
Proverbs 31:10

Ladies, there is no such thing as the perfect man, but if you want to attract the perfect man, you'll need to understand what it means to be a woman of virtue. The Bible outlines the characteristics of the virtuous woman; if you find that you are attracting the wrong type of men, then it's time to look within. Take the time to reflect on who you are and whether you're prepared to take on the following tasks.

Faith: Does God come first in every aspect of your life? For a woman of virtue, God is first in all things, from matters of the heart to her way of thinking, especially when nurturing and strengthening her soul.

Matrimony: How do men view you? When I was in the dating game, I encountered men that were just after sex, but something about me kept them from pursuing me in that way. I've lost count of how many times I was told by a man that they could not go any further with the relationship because they viewed me as the type of woman you bring home to mom and marry. Since they were more focused on sowing their wild oats, they were forced to acknowledge my virtue and step away because they weren't ready for the commitment it would take to grow with me.

Are you the type of woman that can or does respect her husband no matter what? The virtuous woman has such a close relationship with God that she understands that God ultimately has control in all things, so when God's chosen son doesn't behave according to His will, she can step aside to hand him over to the Father for discipline. You will be your husband's helper, not a disciplinarian, nor his mother. Bring him before God in prayer, stand back, and watch the salvation of the Lord! Early in our marriage, I would get so frustrated that I would demand things from my husband because I felt I deserved a certain level of success and maturity from my spouse. When he would fall short, it would annoy me immensely. It wasn't until I realized that I was attempting to do God's job of leading, grooming, and teaching His son, that I stepped aside in repentance to allow the Head of our marriage to take over. It was then that God began to surround my husband with men of honor and strong kingdom relationships. The things I attempted to demand began to flow from him freely, and I took my rightful place as the guard of his heart and his source of encouragement. This also strengthened my husband's trust in me as his wife.

Child Rearing: If you and your spouse have decided that you will raise children together, are you prepared to teach them the ways of God? God has commissioned parents to train up their children in the way they should go, and that path will never depart from them. Are you prepared to instill such wisdom unto your children?

Wedded Bliss: The Five Year Foundation

Raising children is rewarding yet one of the most challenging experiences you may encounter in life. As they attempt to navigate through life, they will have to draw on the things you've taken the time to teach them academically, spiritually, and physically.

Health: In modern times, both husband and wife may provide and prepare family meals, so we'll take a more updated approach in this area. No matter who takes the lead in the kitchen, at least one of you should be taking the time to nurture the family by providing healthy home-cooked meals. Of course, eating out will happen between date nights, family outings, and children's events, but the bulk of your nutritional intake should come from home and should consist of foods that will support healthy living. Even when you eat out, do your best to choose trustworthy restaurants and offer healthy alternatives. You and your spouse want to live a long healthy life together. To enjoy your time with your family to the fullest, you must take care of the temple (body) with which God has blessed you.

Take the time now to consider your current lifestyle and outlook on health. Are you focused on ensuring that you eat to live, or do you live to eat? Are you ensuring that you provide your family with their best start with nutrient-rich food options that boost optimal physical performance? The virtuous woman caters to her family's health, and she ensures that everyone is on task in this department. My husband, like me, was raised by a southern family, which means fried foods, good old cakes baked from scratch, and Sunday dinners that looked like Thanksgiving had rolled around. When we were dating, I would often make dinner for us, and he noticed that, though I come from the same southern background, my meals were healthier. I would joke and tell him if we got married, he'd have to kiss fried foods goodbye because he's not allowed to die early and leave me raising the kids. He valued my concern for his health and has transitioned well to his healthier diet. Yes, we still enjoy those southern meals on occasion, and I can cook them very well, but we do not indulge in these foods daily. It's pleasing to know that my family's health and well-being are right on track.

Finances: I've spoken to many wives over the years and, unless their husbands were exceptionally gifted in this area, the wives were the ones that managed the household finances. My mother handled the finances in our home, and the same was true for my husband's home growing up, which may be why we easily fell into the same roles. He rarely knows what bills are due when, but he knows without a shadow of a doubt that the bills are paid timely, and he knows the weekly budget that we have set for spending. Take a look at how you currently manage your funds.

Do you know where your money goes each month?

Are you left wondering what happened to your check right after you got paid?

Being a good steward of finances is a must for couples. One should possess a healthy understanding that money is nothing more than a resource, a tool used to fuel your goals and create a generational legacy.

Hidden Desires

They seem innocent but create avoid in a marriage. These desires can and will be used by Satan to place a wedge between you and your spouse. Therefore, it's essential to be completely transparent with one another.

These deep desires can arise in the form of intimacy, intelligence, emotional fulfillment, financial gains, health; they can lurk in any part of us and our relationships. If gone unaddressed for too long, you will notice traits in others that fill the void that your spouse seems to neglect. Becoming enticed by these traits lead to an unlawful/forbidden attraction to the object of your infatuation. Note that one can cheat on their spouse with a man, woman, place, or thing; it simply depends on what your hidden desire is.

Consider Adam and Eve being naked in the garden. Everything about themselves was revealed to the other. There were no mysteries between them because they bore no shame until the serpent played on a hidden desire, a piece of fruit!

Eating the forbidden fruit or satisfying one's hidden desire put's you both on the road to distraction. If Adam and Eve had stood together, unveiled their weakness before God, and resisted the devil with the full power bestowed to them, Mankind wouldn't have fallen from grace. Your home together is your Eden, do not get cast out of your garden chasing hidden desires!

Delight yourself in the Lord,

Wedded Bliss: The Five Year Foundation

> and he will give you
> the desires of your heart.
> Psalms 37:4 ESV

That which you desire can be granted to you through your committed relationship with God. Share your deepest selves with one another. Have no shame, no fear, lay down roots within your relationship that make it impossible to uproot your marriage. Whatever department your spouse is falling short in, bring it to God in your corporate prayers (while praying together). Let it be no secrets between you. Watch God begin to mold you both into the man and woman that He's destined you both to be. In this time, you two will begin to fulfill one another in a way that no one else ever could. This is the God marriage, the unbreakable union, the spiritual unicorn of the marriage ministry.

The biblical marriage exists, and it knows no color; it knows no limitations. The power of a couple that humbles themselves and submits to the will and purpose of being united by God possesses the power to change the world. Ye, who are movers of mountains, untouchable by enemies, unstoppable to obstacles, always ahead of the curve. The two joined as one becomes a supernatural force that cannot be easily destroyed. When you look at your spouse, you should feel strength, accomplishment, joy, and sheer awe at what God can, does, and will do through you two.

Perfection In Imperfection

In closing, I want to clarify that a biblical marriage does not imply that everything will be perfect or that the relationship will be one size fits all. It's not all glitter and gold. When you look at relationships in the Bible, you will see that it was what I refer to as a blessed mess. In 1 Samuel 25, we meet Nabal's wife, Abigail. Her husband was wealthy but not exactly a prize spouse. The meaning of his name translates to fool. Abigail successfully saves their household from certain death after her husband mouths off to David's men, provoking his anger. We see wives desperate to provide heirs to their husbands, giving their handmaids in an attempt to fill their duty. We see a king taking the life of a man just to "legally" take his wife. Living according to God's template doesn't make you exempt from trials, woes, or tribulations. Marriage will shine an unwanted light on you that forces you to come to grips with what needs to be purged to become the best version of yourself.

Nevertheless, the two of you will conquer and create, paving the way for generations to come. Your marriage is bigger than the two of you. You are both unique, and each of you carries a gift or anointing that is the answer to someone else's prayer. Be patient with one another, lean on each other, and cherish each other. There will be times when you have no one to count on but your spouse. In time you'll reach a point when no one knows you as well as he or she does, and your comfort will be found in each other's arms. Remember that even when you lose sight of what brought you together, there is a larger plan at play. As you enter or continue in your

Wedded Bliss: The Five Year Foundation

marriage, I pray that you find purpose in one another and that you both accomplish what you were joined together to achieve.

About The Author

Jeniece Drake is a motivational speaker, business coach, TV Show Host, and passionate entrepreneur who enjoys helping people and their businesses grow to reach their full potential. As a life coach, she aims to train, encourage, and help individuals access the resources they need to realize their purpose and attain their goals in life. She understands the rough terrains of life and business, thus dedicates her time and life to assist those she meets in smoothly navigating the rough waters as they strive for success.

Jeniece knows that not everybody is willing to help but takes her gift of serving others as a way of attracting more blessings and spreading optimism wherever she goes. She uses her travel agency to offer more opportunities for growth and enjoying life. She has transformed it into a refuge and safe place for travel professionals who want to take time off the busy and intricate business demands. She offers an escape for those who just want to travel and have fun, as well as those who are seeking a mentor to help them build their travel agencies.

Besides her business, Jeniece is also a co-author of a motivational book, *Manifesting Excellence*, which shares her journey and how she overcame adversity to attain excellence. She holds a B.A. in Applied Behavioral Science and is a Certified Integrative Wellness & Life Coach, besides her other qualifications. Her educational background in behavioral science allows her to understand and connect with people from diverse cultural backgrounds. She respects every culture and individual beliefs and is ready to mingle with everybody. This positive trait allows her to help everyone rise above societal prejudices to embrace their unique individuality. Her next move is to launch her brand as the Multi-Level Marketing (MLM) Slayer, which she plans to use to advance her agenda of coaching business owners to scale up their businesses and break free from the limitations of MLM.

www.ingramcontent.com/pod-product-compliance
Lightning Source LLC
Chambersburg PA
CBHW022110160426
43198CB00008B/428